The Alhambra told to children

Text RICARDO VILLA-REAL

Drawings PILARÍN BAYÉS DE LUNA

Ediciones Miguel Sánchez

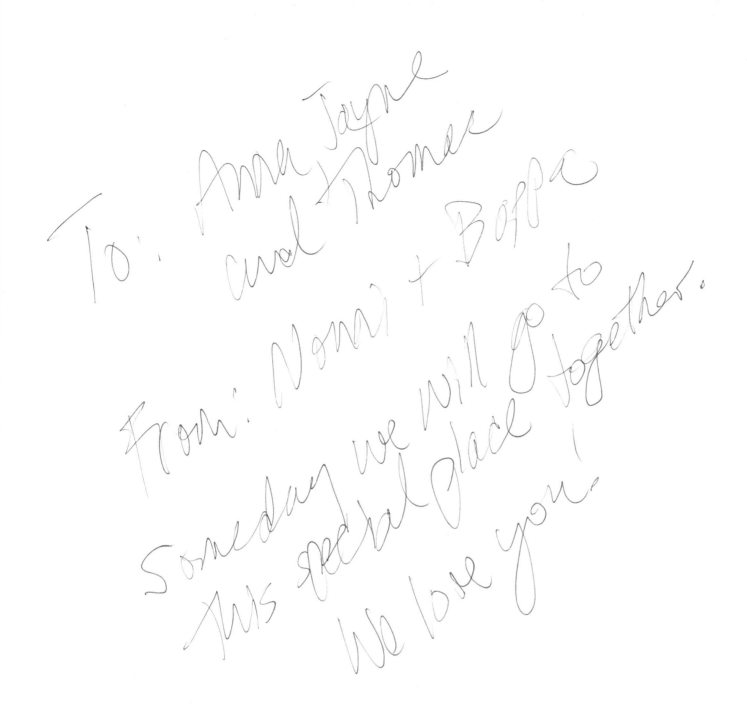

To: Anna Jayne
and Thomas

From: Nona + Boppa

Someday we will go to
this special place together.

We love you!

© of this edition: Ediciones Miguel Sánchez (Marqués de Mondéjar, 44. Granada)

© of the drawings: Pilarín Bayés de Luna

Translation by: René Taylor

Typesetting: Portada, s.l.

Photomechanics: Paperlitos, s.l. (Granada)

Printing: Gracor, S.L. (Móstoles, Madrid)

Legal Deposit: GR-597/1997

I.S.B.N.: 84-7169-053-5

Printed in Spain

The grandfather with his white beard smiles with satisfaction. He has shown the Alhambra and the Generalife to his three grandchildren and to a little friend who is accompanyng them.

They descend through the leafy wood, after the visit, beset by so many emotions. The grandfather contemplates the small face of Pepito who will shortly be ten years old, a face full of gladness. And the sparkling blue eyes of Rosy who has passed her eleventh birthday. The pensive brow of Luisín who is of the same age. And the expression of curiosity and almost of absorption of Juanita, their mutual little friend who is about twelve.

He feels satisfaction at having given of his best to all four of them and planted in their young and innocent hearts the seeds of culture, art and history.

Abruptly Rosy stops and the other with her. Then she speaks: «Grandad, why don't you relate to as many other children as you can all marvellous things that you have been telling us?

The grandfather remains thoughtful for a moment. Then decides that in the measure of his ability he will gratify his granddaughter's wish. And so this was how this brief account was born.

A LITTLE HISTORY

Once upon a time there was, and still is, a city in the south of Spain full of charm and life, of history and art, called Granada. Fine palaces, an imposing cathedral, a fascinating Chapel royal, churches and convents without number, quarters such as the Albaicín, full of streets and alleys, winding and mysterious.

But of all these many monuments, there is one that surpasses them all. I refer to

the Alhambra. Inside its walls the imagination and fancy take wing unchecked. As it is Oriental, whoever visits it dreams of fairies and genii, ogres and hidden treasures, of sultanas and princesses, and mysterious events, just as in *The Thousand and One Nights*.

But look. We aren't dealing now with a fantasy, but reality. We are going to leave dreams behind and are going to describe the Alhambra as it really is. But beforehand it would be very convenient if you were to know something of its history.

As you probably know, Spain has always been invaded by foreign peoples. The Phoenicians and the Greeks came to trade. The Carthaginians came to conquer. The Romans arrived and for centuries they were the country's rulers. Among many other things they gave us

our beautiful language. Then came the Visigoths.

From all these peoples we have inherited endless things, customs even laws and a multitude of words.

At the beginning of the 8th-century the Moors arrived, whose religion is *Islam*. We call them *Moslems, Moham-medans, Saracens*... Owing to their exploits, for they were very brave, they became masters of the whole of Spain, except for a small corner in the north. They were learned and cultivated, and they had their heyday under the Caliphate of Córdoba. But… they fought amongst themselves and against the Christians. And then they lost their sense of unity and split up into a multitude of small independent kingdoms (called *taifas*). And needless to say the Christians took advantage of this to reconquer their lands (kingdoms of Asturias, of León, of Castile, of Navarre, of Aragón…).

One of these Moslem kingdoms was the kingdom of Granada. Here there were two dynasties of *emirs* (or kings), namely the *Zirids* with four monarchs and the *Nazrites* with numerous sultans. These nazrites embellished the cities of their small kingdom, such as Málaga and Almería... But they gave pride of place to Granada. And the most valued jewel that they built and the most cherished was the Alhambra.

THE ALHAMBRA

For the poets the Alhambra is «a crown on the brow of Granada», «a Paradise on earth», «a ruby on the temples of the city», a dream, a treasure of harmony and light... And many other things beside.

But let us leave the poets. What does the word Alhambra mean? It means «red». So that in the Arabic tongue *alqalá al hamra* means the red or russet castle. They say that this name comes from the reddish colour of its towers and ramparts, that with the stars it is silver and with the sun it is changed into gold. The four monarchs who embellished most were Mohammed al-Ahmar and his son in the 13th-century, and in the 14th Yusuf I and his son Mohammed V.

But don't forget, little friends, that the Alhambra was not only a court and palatine residence (*alcazar* in Arabic), but also a fortress for the purpose of defense (in Arabic *alcazaba*) and even a small township (in Arabic *medina*).

Gate of Justice. The magnificient gateway giving access to the Alhambra is called *The Gate of Justice* (or more accurately *Gate of the Esplanade*). It is, as you can see, very imposing, tinged with orange and gold. Now look closely and don't let this next detail escape you. On the first horseshoe arch, the outer one, you can see a very large hand (probably a talisman or a good luck charm) that has been carved there. And in the second and smaller arch a key has been sculptured, which signifies power and authority.

A charming centuries-old legend tells us that beneath this gateway there is a gorgeous palace, no less, and that in it dwell an Arab astrologer who has cast a spell over a captive Christian princess with blue eyes and fair hair. The spell will one day be broken and then, alas!, the hand will sieze the key and the Alhambra will vanish.

Square of the Cisterns. This square or esplanade is called *of the Aljibes* because beneath it there exist deposits holding large supplies of good cool water. A small kiosk, a well… For centuries the people of Granada have drunk and enjoyed this water, transported down into the city by the water –sellers, almost always on the backs of donkeys.

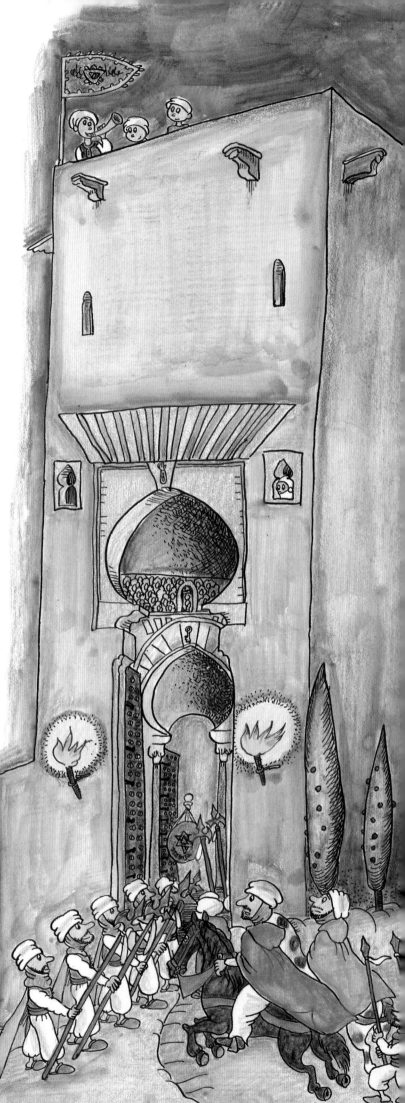

Once upon a time, so the story goes, there was a water– seller called Peregil. A good and compassionate man, he lent assistance at the side of this very well to a poor Moor who was very sick and took him into his own house. In gratitude the Moor gave him a parchment and a candle, made up of strange ingredients. Later on, armed with these strange artifacts, Peregil would discover a great treasure in the vaults of the Tower of the Seven Floors…

CARLOS V

On the right-hand side of the square there stands an attractive Gate called *The Wine Gate* with a charming coupled window and once more the mysterious key. Also on the right is the splendid **Palace of Charles V**. Facing us is the quarter of the city called the Albaicín, which we shall see better later on. On the left there stands a formidable array of towers. This is the *Alcazaba*.

The Alcazaba. The word alcazaba means a fortress, a defensive castle, invariably perched on the top of a hill or bluff. Its purpose was to protect the palace and the city. All over this territory there

were watch-towers or *atalayas*. If some peril were to be discovered, flames or bonfires by night or a thick column of smoke by day notified and gave warning. It was rather like what you have seen the indians do in movies of the Wild West. At the entrance is the lovely garden of the *Adarves* (*adarve* is the pathway on top of a fortress).

Round a corner and down a passageway… and there stands the **Tower of la Vela**. Here means *watchfulness* and *vigilance*, in other words, sentinels and guards. It is the loftiest of all the towers (such as those of Arms and Homage). In wonder our eyes contemplate in all four directions a marvellous and unique view. A poet has said:

Give him alms, woman,
For life holds no greater affliction
Than that of being
Blind in Granada.

As we are not blind, thanks be to God, we are able to enjoy the contemplation or of the river Darro, deep down below our parapet, or the view of the **Albaicín**, one of the world's most famous quarters, so white, with its diminutive houses hemmed in one against the other, and its *cármenes*, its churches and convents, its small intimate squares and winding streets… Or the view of the Vega where one's gaze becomes lost in the distant horizon, or the city at our feet, or the snowy peaks of the Sierra Nevada, the highest in the Spanish Peninsula, or…, but what do I know? The Tower of la Vela and its bell are symbols fot the people of Granada. And we remember the verses:

> *I want to live in Granada*
> *If only to hear*
> *The bell of La Vela*
> *To lull me off to sleep.*

Do you know, my little friends –how funny— that the girls and unmarried young women of Granada touch the bell on certain times of the year to avoid remaining single?

THE ROYAL HOUSE

This is the name given to the palaces of the Alhambra. As in all Oriental palaces, their interiors are divided fundamentally into three departments. And each department has its corresponding and surrounding structures. The three departments which we are going to enjoy are, including both their Spanish and Arabic names, the following: **The Golden Room (Mexuar)**, the **Room of Comares** (the official court) and the **Room of the Lions (Harem)**. In the first justice was dispensed, in the second all political and diplomatic activity took place and in the third the kings led their private lives.

MEXUAR. "Enter and you will find justice". This was the inscription on a ceramic tile that was once encrusted in the wall. "Enter and make your plea. Don't be afraid to ask for justice, for it is here that you will find it".

Step by step we have come into a delightful gallery or portico, a beautiful and well-tendend garden (called "of Machuca", because these were the living quartiers of the architect who built the palace of the emperor Charles V). A small pool…, and many flowers.

The chamber. Don't be confused if you see that some Christian motifs have been placed here. Most precious are the *arabesques* (adornments of leaves and designs), the four slender columns, the beautiful stucco decoration (which is white gypsum with liquid glue), the *alicatados* (ceramic tiles). At the end of the chamber there is a little *oratory*. It is singularly beautiful and bears the following inscription: "Come and pray". There are several small coupled windows, that is separated or divided by means of a slender column called a *parteluz* or mullion. (Some people improperly refer to it as an *ajimez*).

And now the courtyard. But first a word of advice. From now onwards, when you are not under the open sky but in chambers and halls, look up first at the ceiling, whether or not it be an *artesonado*, that is richly worked. And do you know why? This is simply because the Moslems cherished them greatly and almost all of them are an enchantment.

This courtyard is small and its columns have strange capitals. In the centre there is a lovely marble basin. The façade is of outstanding beauty: arabesques, small windows, latticework, a frieze of carved wood, a grand cornice. Here is an amusing anecdote. The people of Granada with a certain wit say that the marble of the door on the right, which seems to be warped, is so because they cut it while it was still green!

THE ROOM OF COMARES. Here everyone stands open-mouthed. It is only natural. The **Court of the Arrayanes**. Do you know what *arrayán* is? It is an Arabic word which is equivalent to our word *myrtle*, which is a sweet-smelling plant or bush.

This court, rectangular and with a pool, is the centre of the royal palace, which some call the *seraglio*, an Arabic or Persian word,

which is always confused with *harem*. The latter, as we shall see, was the family or private residence of the Moslem kings.

As you see, it has a great pool in the middle, lined with myrtle hedges and with rooms at both sides. From the southern portico we can imagine kings from abroad and foreign envoys stunned with astonishment, while the granadine monarch, seated on his throne under the beautiful *Tower of Comares*, waits to receive them. Slowly, so as to intensify our pleasure, we move towards the other portico, the columns, ceilings and arches of *mocárabes* (that is to say stalactites, enrichments which hang downwards and invariably take the form of an inverted pyramid). On the walls those strange signs that we see are the characters of Arabic script. There are pious prayers and poems, and amongst them, much repeated, as it is all over the Alhambra, is the motto of the nazrite kings: "God alone is victorious".

Hall of the Barca. At each side of the entrance are two niches or alcoves or small closets which people refer to as *babucheros*. But it is not true that they were meant to hold *babuchas* or slippers, but rather lamps, pitchers of water or small pots of flowers. And why do they call it of the Barca? Some people, and they too are off the mark, say that it derives from its beautiful roof, which resembles the keel of a *barca* or boat upside down. In fact, it comes from an arabic word, *baraka*, meaning a blessing of greeting.

We are now in the throne room. It is called the **Hall of Ambassadors** and occupies the admirable interior of the great Tower of Comares (in Arabic *comarias* are stained-glass windows). How grand it is! There are nine rooms with their corresponding balconies. In the middle the monarch's throne supposedly stood, directly facing the patio.

No, I'm not surprised that once again you stand enthralled, as you admire the roofing of the hall and the vault that covers it with its dome of cedar wood, its small windows, its friezes of arabesques and *mocárabes*, and its tiny stars.

Before going on further, I want to tell you something of history. It is of the greatest interest and I'm sure that it will enlighten you very considerably.

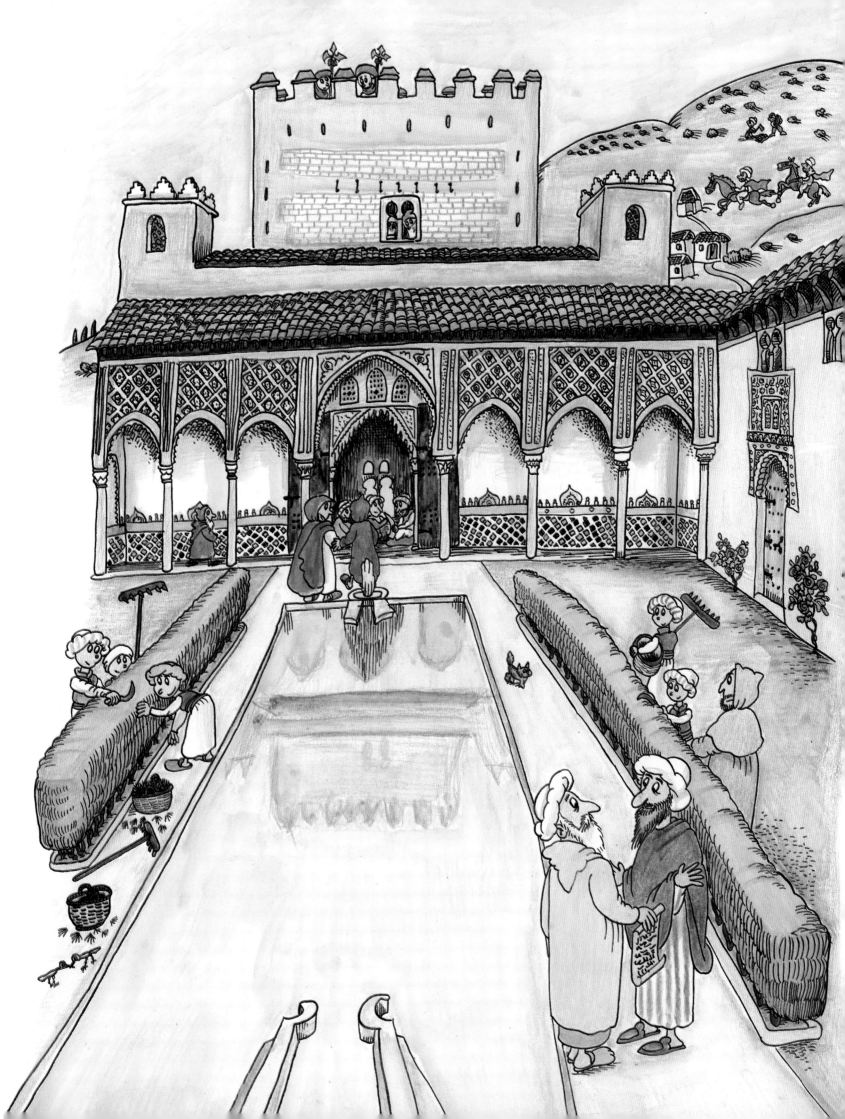

Hassan's brother and therefore Boabdil's uncle. The Moslems of Granada did get on among themselves, but killed each other off.

What happened was that Abul Hassan repudiated Fatima "la Horra" so as to replace her as favourite by a Christian captive, Isabel de Solis, whom the granadinos called Zoraya. He despised and hated his son Boabdil, and tried to murder him. The Christians nicknamed Boabdil *El Rey Chico*, the Little King (because he did not wield as much power as his father). In their turn his subjects dubbed him *El Zogoibi*, which means "the luckless one", the poor little fellow.

Abul Hassan died and for sure, according to tradition, ordered that he should be buried among the

BOABDIL, THE LAST KING OF GRANADA.

From one of these balconies in the Hall of Ambassadors which give out on to the river Darro, queen Fatima, called *Aixa la Horra* (the honest queen), let down her son Boabdil to save him from certain death. For you must know that when the Catholic Kings, Ferdinand of Aragon and Isabella of Castile, were besieging the city, after having conquered almost the entire Nazrite kingdom, there were in the latter no less than three kings. The first, Muley Abul Hassan (known to the Christians as Mulhacén). The second was his son Boabdil, who had rebelled against him. And the third was known as El Zagal, which in arabic means "the courageous one". He was everlasting snows of the Sierra Nevada (Mulhacén, as you know, is the tallest mountain of the Peninsula). El Zagal having been defeated and banished, Boabdil remained as sole king. First a captive, then freed and later on exiled, Boabdil signed in the Hall of Ambassadors the surrender and delivery of Granada and the Alhambra.

What happened next? Well, according to tradition it happened in a place since called *The Sigh of the Moor*. But rather than letting me tell it you, read the ballad of that time that recounts it as follows:

From a lofty slope
Granada lay before him.
He gazed once more at Granada
And spoke after this fashion:
Oh, Granada, the far-famed,
My solace and my joy!
Oh, my lofty Albaicin
And my rich Alcaicería!
Oh, my Alhambra and my domains
And my precious mosque!
My baths, gardens and rivers,
Where I would take my ease…
For yesterday I was a famous king
And today I have nothing of my own…
His mother rode ahead of him
With other cavaliers;
Seeing the people motionless,
The queen, too, halted,
And she asked the reason why
Because she was unaware.
An elderly Moor answered her
With honest courtesy:
—Your son weeps for Granada
And he is afflicted with grief.
His mother gave this answer
And after this fashion spoke:
—It is well that as a woman
He weeps in great anguish,
He, who as knight should,
Did not defend his estate.

Besides the queen mother, others in this melancholy train on their way to exile included Moraima, Boabdil's wife, and their sons. Boabdil lived for a short time in the Alpujarra mountains. Then he went off to Africa, where he lived and died in obscurity.

CHAMBER OF THE LIONS (HAREM). A most beautiful court, a marvel of delicacy, the **Court of the Lions**, which you will have admired so many times in photographs and engravings. Well, you are now in it.

As we have said before, this courtyard with its structures and dependencies constitutes the Harem. Here the emir lived his domestic and family life, far from the bustle and commitments of the court.

Here there is much to see and much to talk about. Yes, my little friends. First of all…, how shall I put it? You need to establish in your imagination some comparisons. For example, it looks like a grove of 124 palm-trees, for this is what the columns resemble. It seems like an oasis in the desert, disposed around the central fountain with its twelve lions. It resembles the cloister of a monastery with its pavilions of three arches. It resembles… (but let your own imagination take wing).

The fountain of marble rests on the backs of the lions. The water, so much loved by

the arabs, shoots up and flows from the basin to the moths of the beasts and from there makes its way in all directions. Round the rim of the basin a poem (*qasida* in Arabic) tells us amongst other things that the water, "pearls of translucent brightness", is "liquid silver that runs among the jewels", and prevents the lions, lacking life, to give vent to their ferocity.

Hall of the Abencerrajes. It is on the south side of the patio. It is famous for its beauty… and the legend that becomes confused with history. This is because it was here that numerous knights of the illustrious family of the Abencerrajes (a word which in Arabic signifies *Sons of the saddler*) were executed on the orders of the cruel Muley Abul Hassan, because they were partisans of Boabdil and his mother, as also of El Zagal.

But let us look at some of the details of this room: the door that provides access to it with its wonderful decorations, the exquisite starred dome, the sixteen small windows, so very lovely, the socles (which in Arabic are called *almatrayas*), the two alcoves and the basin of white marble. And what do we see in it? Some stains that look like blood. Can these be traces of the executions? No and again no, my friends. The truth is that they are the ochre oxidation of the marble. Of course, in no corner of the Alhambra is it possible to escape from fantasy.

The Hall of the Kings. This chamber or more exactly long gallery, occupying the east side of the courtyard, is called the *Hall of the Kings* and rather more inapropiately of *Justice*. It is very curious. Look carefully now. Doesn't is seem like a theatre? It is so very long, divided into sections by means of six wonderful arches, three porticoes and the arches double and encrusted with *mocárabes*. At each end is an alcove.

Do you know something? In this hall the first Mass was celebrated after the Catholic Kings had gained possession of Granada and the Alhambra. Imagine in this very place the court, the knights… Luxury, arms, banderoles and standards… Yes, and in one small corner, alone and isolated, stood an unknown person among the kings, princes nobles, soldiers and clerics. Do you know who he was? Well, Christopher Columbus, no less. Yes, my small friends. The future discoverer of the New World had waited patiently for the kings to enter the city, so as later on to sign in Santafé the capitulations of the Discovery.

You will ask me: "Well, but why is it called *of the Kings*? Very simple. It is because of the painting on the ceiling of one of the small side alcoves representing ten Nazrite kings. And in the other two recesses there are also paintings of freat charm depicting scenes of hunting, tournaments, castles and even a game of chess.

Hall of the Two Sisters and Mirador of Daraxa. On the north side of the Court of the Lions is the Hall of the Two Sisters. No, don't dream of legends and fantasies. The two mysterious sisters are the two great marble flagstones on each side of the fountain in the middle and its spout. (An odd remark: it has been said, and it is true, that the Arabs who love water so much like it to flow like a whisper, almost silently and humbly, making the least noise).

Yes, I understand. Once more you stand gaping in wonder. A marvellous dome, enchantment unlimited, radiance, beautiful ornament wrought by means of tiles and *atauriques* (Oriental work, carved or painted, inspired in vegetable motifs). And everywhere the socle of tiles, a poem of praise. A small room next to it is called *of the Ajimeces*. In its centre is the *Mirador of Daraxa*, which served as the queen's bedchamber.

People call it *Lindaraja*, the same name they use for the court below, but *daraxa* means "the queen's house". It has a socle of small painted tiles that is a marvel. The windows are placed low, because you must know the Moslem custom in to recline on cushions at floor level. In this way you got a better view of the landscape, hidden in later times by other rooms of the *Court of Lindaraja*.

The Baths. The Arabs were very clean and hygienic. They loved water and the bath. This, a Moslem palace, couldn't be without them. The first room, called the *Room of Repose* or *of the Beds* would have been the last to be used, after passing through other rooms and bathing tanks with hot and cold water, and a room for taking steam baths (today we call them *saunas*). Then to rest. For this reason we see water containers, niches or beds, which in those days would have been furnished with rugs and curtains. Can you imagine what the Alhambra must have looked like with furniture and curtains everywhere?

GARDENS OF EL PARTAL AND THE TOWERS. Light and colour, and every variety of dazzling hue. And trees, shrubs, flowers and water everywhere. This is *El Partal* (or pórtico).

Ramparts and many towers. I'll now tell you their names. The first, with its great pool, is the *Tower of the Ladies*. Next there comes a small prayer room. Then the *Tower of the Spikes*, and then that of the *Cadi* (which in Arabic means *judge*). Some people, what a joke!, say *del Candil* or Oil-lamp. Further on is the *Tower of the Fair Captive,* because, so they say, it was here that Isabel de Solis or Zoraya lived. Next is the *Tower of the Infantas*. Don't fail to go into it. It is the cutest thing, a toy. It has certainly given rise to various tales or legends. I can now remember two. That of the three beautiful princesses, Zaida, Zoraida and Zorahaida, and the three Christian knights who were captives, and that of the "Rosa of the Alhambra" who with her magic lute and wonderful voice relieved and cured no less a person than king Philip V of his bewitchment and depressión. There we go! The remaining towers are of less interest and link up with the Gate of Justice.

THE GENERALIFE

Garden of gardens. "A Garden beyond compare". It is true. The Generalife is the most famous garden in Spain. Well, if you press me, it is amongst the most famous gardens in the world. Gardens and more gardens, and orchards, recumbent or hanging from a slope. It was... shall I tell you? A royal

almunia (in Arabic a garden), a house of relaxation for the emirs.

If we want to know what Generalife means, we run into a bit of trouble. For some it means "house of delight" for others "garden of Eden". The truth, and I'm not taking you in, is that it derives from "garden of the *alarife*" (This Arabic word is equivalent to architect or master builder).

We enter into the *Paseo of the Cypresses*, slender and tall. Next the *Garden* or *Paseo of the Oleanders*, with vaults of flowers and shrubbery. And look! here is the world-famous *Patio of the Acequia* or the Long Pool, with its jets of water, rectangular in shape and between constructions. The patio has two porticoes. In one of them, so the story goes, prince Ahmed al Kamel, whom they called "The Pilgrim of Love", was confined (all this is according to a charming legend). He had learned the language of birds and being lonely made friends with a bat, a swallow, a hawk, some nightingales and a faithful dove. But, of course, his favourites were an owl and a parrot. They helped him woo a Christian princess, whom he maried. On becoming king, the grateful prince named the owl his prime minister and the parrot his master of ceremonies. You can read this and many other

legends in the beautiful *Tales of the Alhambra* by Washington Irving.

Next to the Court of the Pool is the *Court of the Cypresses* or *the Sultana*, because, according to tradition, a queen once hid herself in the trunk of one of these trees. There are also the *Upper Gardens* with their *Stairway of the Cascades*, down whose banisters the water rushes. There are also the *New Gardens*, because they are of recent date, with their rose-bowers, pergolas, flowers and water everywhere, and even an open-air theatre.

* * *

When you have finished seeing all these wonders, repeat within yourselves: I must go back! I must go back!

And here's an end to the tale…

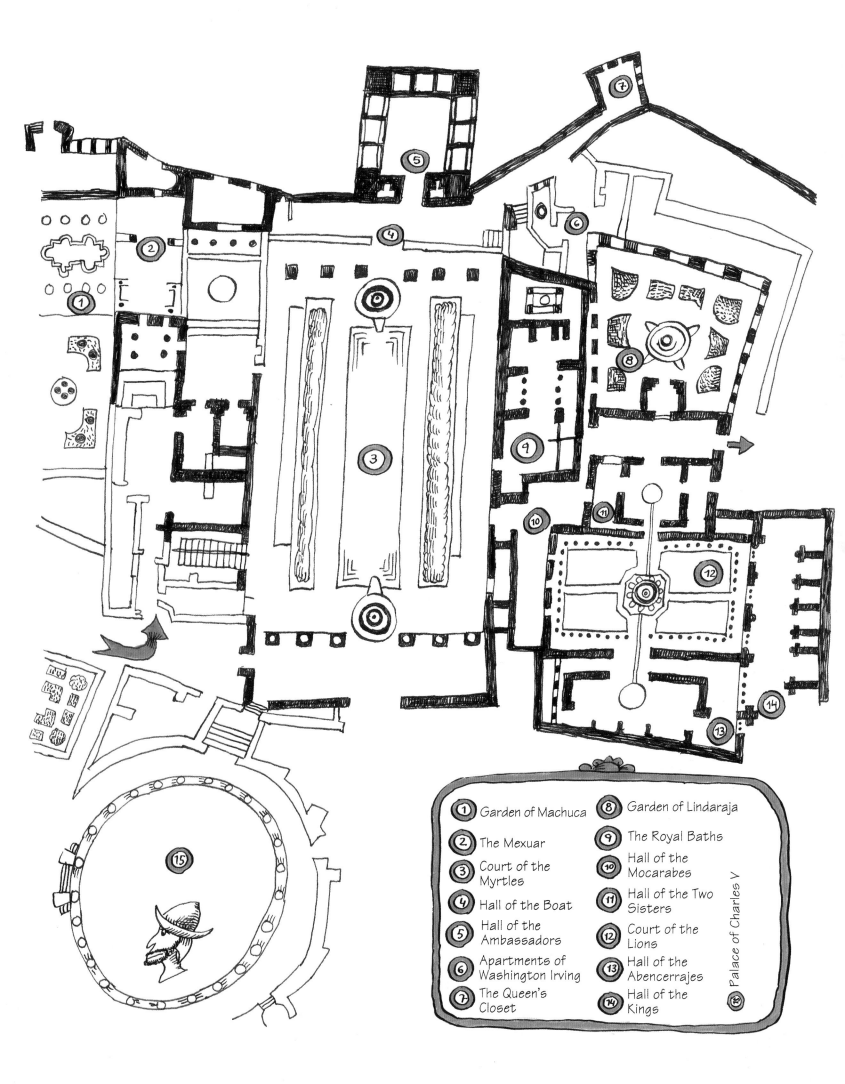

1. Garden of Machuca
2. The Mexuar
3. Court of the Myrtles
4. Hall of the Boat
5. Hall of the Ambassadors
6. Apartments of Washington Irving
7. The Queen's Closet
8. Garden of Lindaraja
9. The Royal Baths
10. Hall of the Mocarabes
11. Hall of the Two Sisters
12. Court of the Lions
13. Hall of the Abencerrajes
14. Hall of the Kings
15. Palace of Charles V